Itty Bitty Animals

ITTY BITTY TREE FROGS

By Gunner Quick

Gareth Stevens Publishing

Please visit our website, www.garethstevens.com. For a free color catalog of all our high-quality books, call toll free 1-800-542-2595 or fax 1-877-542-2596.

Library of Congress Cataloging-in-Publication Data

Quick, Gunner.
Itty bitty tree frogs / by Gunner Quick.
p. cm. — (Itty bitty animals)
Includes index.
ISBN 978-1-4339-9896-6 (pbk.)
ISBN 978-1-4339-9897-3 (6-pack)
ISBN 978-1-4339-9894-2 (library binding)
1. Hylidae — Juvenile literature. 2. Tree frogs. 3. Frogs. I. Title.
QL668.E24 Q53 2014
597.878—dc23

First Edition

Published in 2014 by
Gareth Stevens Publishing
111 East 14th Street, Suite 349
New York, NY 10003

Editor: Ryan Nagelhout
Designer: Nicholas Domiano

Photo credits: Cover, pp.1, 5, 9, 13, 19, 23, 24 (feet, leaves) iStockphoto/Thinkstock.com; p. 7 Heiko Kiera/ Shutterstock.com; p. 11 Eduard Kyslynskyy/Shutterstock.com; p. 15 Bianca Lavies/National Geographic/Getty Images; p. 17 Brandon Alms/Shutterstock.com; p. 21 Photodisc/Thinkstock.com.

Printed in the United States of America

CPSIA compliance information: Batch #CW14GS: For further information contact Gareth Stevens, New York, New York at 1-800-542-2595.

Contents

Tree frogs are tiny!

They live in trees.

They are very light.
They can move
on top of leaves.

Their long legs help them jump.

They have very sticky feet. These help them climb.

Green tree frogs love to eat flies.

Red-eyed frogs sleep during the day.

Gray tree frogs
can change color!
They can turn green.

Some are toxic!
These are called
poison dart frogs.

Their many bright colors
tell other animals
to stay away!

Words to Know

feet

leaves

Index